Advance Praise for *Clothesline Religion*

"How fierce and resilient, what a tremendous and tender heart. *Clothesline Religion* is gorgeous, powerful. I was utterly enrapt, reading it out in the yard under the full sun. And transformed—the book inspired me to take my own daughter out of school for a road trip, time for just her and I. Mother and daughter."
—Robin MacArthur, author of *Half Wild*

"*Clothesline Religion* offers each reader a chance to hang out in the opened air with the extraordinary Megan Buchanan. Each poem has a lived-in magic, longing transformed by candor, and candor, by music."
—Verandah Porche, author of *Sudden Eden*

"We need to coin a word for the feeling that happens when I read these poems. It's singular and ecstatic and huge. It's in my chest, near my heart. It makes me want to yell, but instead I remain silent and still inside of it, this feeling. I could stay here forever."
—Rachel Yoder, editor of *draft*, author of *Infinite Things All At Once*

"Megan Buchanan finds the sacred in the everyday and offers poems as fierce evidence, each one 'naked as a hot pancake.' This collection reminds us that the inevitable heartbreaks of being a person can provoke a more vivid awareness of the world around us, so that we see 'the kid/across the teeter-totter' and witness the hummingbirds' 'last sips before flying back to cacti in bisbee.' What could be more enviable that to be 'entirely possessed/by an ordinary magic'?"
—Matthew Burgess, PhD, author of *Slippers for Elsewhere*
and Enormous Smallness: A Story of E. E. Cummings

"Megan Buchanan manages to pack lines with beauty while simultaneously honing them to a sharp, succinct edge. Her work has sinew and muscle and yet extends an open hand."
—Tim McKee, director of publishing, North Atlantic Books

CLOTHESLINE RELIGION

CLOTHESLINE
RELIGION

POEMS

MEGAN BUCHANAN

for Duncan —
spirit brother!
so glad we met
(thank you
John Daly)
with love & gratitude
~ Megan

GREEN WRITERS PRESS *Brattleboro, Vermont*

Printed in the United States

10 9 8 7 6 5 4 3 2 1

Green Writers Press is a Vermont-based publisher
whose mission is to spread a message of hope and
renewal through the words and images we publish.
Throughout we will adhere to our commitment to
preserving and protecting the natural resources of the
earth. To that end, a percentage of our proceeds will
be donated to environmental activist groups. Green
Writers Press gratefully acknowledges support from
individual donors, friends, and readers to help support
the environment and our publishing initiative.

GReen
wriTers
press

Giving Voice to Writers & Artists Who Will Make the World a Better Place
Green Writers Press | Brattleboro, Vermont
www.greenwriterspress.com

ISBN: 978-0996897396

The italicized phrase in "Naked Lady"
comes from *A Midsummer Night's Dream*.

Author and cover photograph by Duncan Johnson.
Author and daughter photograph by Pat McLaughlin
(Derry City, Northern Ireland, 1997).

PRINTED ON PAPER WITH PULP THAT COMES FROM FSC-CERTIFIED FORESTS, MANAGED FORESTS
THAT GUARANTEE RESPONSIBLE ENVIRONMENTAL, SOCIAL, AND ECONOMIC PRACTICES BY
LIGHTNING SOURCE. ALL WOOD PRODUCT COMPONENTS USED IN BLACK & WHITE, STANDARD
COLOR, OR SELECT COLOR PAPERBACK BOOKS, UTILIZING EITHER CREAM OR WHITE BOOKBLOCK
PAPER, THAT ARE MANUFACTURED IN THE LAVERGNE, TENNESSEE PRODUCTION CENTER ARE
SUSTAINABLE FORESTRY INITIATIVE® (SFI®) CERTIFIED SOURCING.

ACKNOWLEDGMENTS

Thanks to the editors of the following publications where some of these poems have previously appeared:

A Woman's Thing: The Wild Issue

Dream Closet: Meditations on Childhood Space

The Sun Magazine

make/shift

Eating Her Wedding Dress: An Anthology of Poems About Clothing

lines+stars

San Pedro River Review

PoemCity 2015/2016, Montpelier, VT

Poem Town 2015/2016, Randolph, VT

Flying Object Press Gallery Show

The Collared Peccary: Poetry of Northern Arizona

The Noise: Flagstaff's Art + News Magazine

Mom Egg Review: Literature + Art

for my relatives

the living

and the dead

and especially

for Gráinne

daughter most alive

CONTENTS

Author's Note

THE POEMS in this collection span the years between 1992 and 2016. I became a mother at twenty-two, working my way through undergrad and grad school, moving around, finding my way.

I crawled out of the warm bed I shared with my daughter— or now, my son—in the deep darkness to write many of these poems. Some of them hurt coming out. Some of them I caught on the breeze.

I read somewhere last year that children can carry the burden of their parents' unrealized dreams. Heavy. This information inspired and propelled me to, among other things, finally gather these poems into the collection that you now hold in your hands.

Arranging them into groups chronologically or geographically (Ireland, California, Arizona, New England), while perhaps making the most logical sense, didn't work for mysterious reasons. There's just something magical about the ABCs, and these poems were happy to line up alphabetically.

A gigantic, heart-exploding thank you to my friends, teachers, students and family. Your belief in me as an artist is medicinal and means the world.

Special thanks to the following people for their loving spirit-support and encouragement: Megan Bathory-Peeler, Bill Batty, Heather Bernard, Avery Buchanan Cherry, Patrick Buchanan, Ryan Buchanan, Timothy Buchanan, Matthew Burgess, Dan Cherry, Matt Cherry, Robin Craig, Barbara Darwall Collins, David and Gail Demaine, Julia Demmin, Lyedie Geer, Jean Gobillot, Marge Gomez, Glenda Gray, Ann Hackler, Frederica Hall, James Jay, Duncan Johnson, Jane Karras, Kristin Kiefer, Diane Kordick, Jayne Lee, Robin MacArthur, Katherine Magistrale, Cortney Manix, Julie Merrill, Moya Kordick Mitchell, Tim McKee, Brian Morgan, Delisa Myles, Tony and Sue Norris, Jody and Chris O'Connor, Lillis O'Laoire, Rachel Onuf, Krishena Bishop Peters, Verandah Porche, Doug Richmond, Saint Rosner, Audrey Sheats, Jim Simmerman, Jeff Solomon, Jessica Star, Chip Stuckmeyer, Rick and Alexandra Taketa, Bonny Van de Kamp, Karen Van de Kamp, Kathleen Van de Kamp, the Vermont Studio Center, Ruth and John Henry Waddell, Zee Wendell, Diana Whitney, Dillon Williamson and Rachel Yoder.

A deep bow of gratitude to Dede Cummings; this book wouldn't exist without her.

Estarás como siempre en alguna frontera
jugándote en tu sueño lindo y desvencijado

You will always be at some border
taking risks in your lovely ragged dream

—MARIO BENEDETTI

CLOTHESLINE RELIGION

A NEW AND FERVENT DOMESTICITY
HAS SEIZED ME

okay, I can understand
the boiling pots of strawberries for jam,
these herbs in the window, gray and green,
my daughter's knees like apples
scrubbed with almond soap,
stacks of white cotton diapers
and
my reverence for clotheslines
has been around for years

but this
ironing
of tea towels
in the dark at half-past one?
scrubbing out the fridge (thumb-
nail detail) two weeks in a row?
I can out-sweep Cinderella,
I'm suspicious of the dishwasher
and I have mastered
all the dagger and caterpillared attachments
of the vacuum

this is inexcusable,
this pressing of creases in myself,
new mother,
this filling up of all my free moments
with tidying, scrubbing,
folding and refolding

as if untidiness was the reason
he didn't want us

as if
I wasn't clean

AGUS AR AIS ARÍS GO hÉIRINN
(and back again to Ireland)

It's Middle Night. I'm trying to read Eavan Boland by closet-light.
How can such a tiny loaf of daughter
take up an entire queen-sized bed?
She's frozen, out, mid cartwheel, heels
four inches from my head.

But that's not all: a mosquito's a-hum, so tiny—
a line drawing of itself!

I hear a tiny motor
inside the mattress, wonder if
the new neighbors downstairs
have a 24-hour can opener.

O the hum and stillness of this night—
my sleeping child, now diagonal
across the down and cotton covers.
She sighs, a perfect little porpoise body,
so miraculous,
hair soft as moths.
Now is sweet—
but what fills the nights of our home-to-be
back across the Atlantic?

Rain and the sea, clouds close as the pillow
that banks my baby from the bed's sudden edge.

Recent nights of fever and dread—
were mosquitoes the only thing to fear
in the home ahead—instead
dampness and war, the fists of my child's father
and the salt spray of failure.

ALMOST–SPRING IN EVERYONE

At dawn, aspen shimmer brandnew beneath dreaming blue peaks.
One heart speaks in beats against another's spine, bright as forest fire.

O holy breakfasts, potatoes and coffee, bacon.
In this new dream, we climb trees, rock faces, crisscross railroad yards
to later find spring water singing in our first language.

The old stone carver leans through coffee's blue steam, whispers this:
beneath our skins lives animal nature, visible to him.
Recognition lifts me like a kite.

A flowered crown lifts off the ground, carried south by a crow,
released onto a rooftop.
A blue heeler and my longlegged child dream in quilts below the tiles.

His long gaze, a hero's name, stronglegged gait down gravel alleyways.
A daydream folded inside my leather boot, wrapped tight in a wing
of blue feathers.

Blue evenings, I find answers in rainclouds, runes made of cinders
or in complete strangers.
A baby leans over her father's shoulder, slowly
raises a hand, anointing me.

ARCHETYPE STUDY #1: MOTHER

Flax meal, omega vites, clean hands,
clean sheets, clean floors, clean
lines of communication.
Quick apologies. Muffins.
Grateful for baby blood tests
negative for lead.
Let the baby sleep
with me in the bed.
Why would anyone
wish to miss
chubby legs
kicking off blankets?
How could I ever
skip the rosy
mornings with baby
waking up and saying *Hi*
or the nights
saying *Moon?*

AVERY MAKES IT NEW

brave as water
calm as butter
dizzy as a smoothie
emblematic as overalls
fresh as a whisker
gentle as a flipflop
hungry as a monkey
icky as a bandaid
jumpy as a brother
keen as a button
loud as toast
merry as mistletoe
naked as a hot pancake
old as a golden ticket
peaceful as oatmeal
quick as macaroni
rich as cinnamon
stubborn as a fiddle
tiny as a tooth
upset as plaid
vivid as thunder
wise as boots
xciting as a sidewalk
yin as milk
zealous as a cornfield, my boy

BABU

There lives a dog that you should know.
And before they cut off his balls,
twice daily he crossed two spring-fed rivers
and forged through miles of cottonwood valley
and cindery cedar plateau
to meet a springer spaniel bitch in heat.
Hard to imagine when you see him now?
Look at him. Can you picture him
far in the distance? At first you think
it might be a sheep, but no. His tail gives him away.

He welcomed me onto the ranch
where I now work, standing very still
or swishing limbs through warm air
while the blue-eyed octogenarian artist
creates mysterious and startling wax replicas of me.
That first morning as I pulled up at the foundry
Babu was waiting by the woodpile.
He lead me through a maze of manzanita,
down seven stone staircases
and across a sleeping orchard.
He turned right at the cottonwood,
its yellow leaves rustling like taffeta
and sat before the invisible fifteen-foot door.
He brought me right to the people
waiting with steaming buckets of wax
and a pot of strange tea, the people
who were waiting for me.

On winter mornings,
the great dog, Babu, and I stand
warm in our spotted skins together

on the concrete studio floor, grateful
for the little black woodstove
and the radiant heat rising up
from copper pipes in the floor.
Babu is fifteen. With a fragrant sigh
he rolls out for a stifflegged nap
beside a bronze woman molded by his master.
Say his name in pig-latin (*Abu-bay*) and his thick tail thumps.
If only I could kiss his wet nose and he become a man.

O Babu, my brother, skin and skin
when my passions are through
I will be ash and air in the cottonwoods.

THE BOATS OF JEROME

Ever notice
how many old boats are nestled
up amongst the rusted pickups and apricot trees
and inbetween the crumbling stone walls
of Jerome, coppermine mountain town
smack in the center of Arizona?
Boats, dozens of them, like grasshoppers
in my late-summer garden—
once your eyes adjust, they're everywhere.
Boats that don't get out much, boats
beached all over town, sleeping
in the shade of rosebushes
planted by whores dead one hundred years.
Boats out back of bars that stink like Ireland,
roasting meat and generations of booze
spilt into carpet, bars full of people
easily turned to pirates. (Last Halloween
I danced with them; I was Hester Prynne.)

Sailboat, rowboat, motorboat, canoe.
Scorpion, broken glass, rattlesnake, booze.

I know of one secret waterfall
where spring water pours like fiddle music
through three old crashed-up cars
nosedived off the clifftop before my grandfather was born.
But no boats travel that crooked stream.

Picture this: someday, as in a dream—
the Verde River takes a deep breath
and rises, swells her cottonwood banks
and on that day

the people of Jerome will be ready!
Hair in braids, flasks filled and loaves
of homemade bread stashed
deep in backpacks. A few will be armed
and some will be praying
but the boats will all be filled
and all the boats will hold.

BRACK / *BREAC*
for Liam Fitzgerald (1977-2003)

The trick is to use tea leaves, so they say,
for raisins and brown sugar overnight
to soak in. Steep one cup of cold gold *tae*
and on the morrow, whether close or bright

you find the sky, the raisins, they won't care.
Two cups of flour, the egg still warm (for luck),
fat spoon of marmalade and once the rare
gift Liam brought me, brown egg of a duck

I whisked in. O I never will forget
sweet richness of that loaf and butter thick
across it, how copper curls from wet
miles crowned his face. Through steam he took a drink

from favorite white enamel mug. Although
still now I bake this bread, the method true
was written hasty by dear Mrs. O
that afternoon I said goodbye and flew

away (for reasons not told now). Too fast
I'm gone from kitchens, gentle warmth of flames
off turf, away from quiet roads and cats
that knew me, lovers in out of the rain.

BUTTERMILK MOON

buttermilk
moon spilling into sky
up over folded mountain ridge
lush evergreen ridge spilling down
to river buttermilk moon rising full
over valley light sliding shimmer–
green water shivering dreamy
cool buttermilk moonlight
golden riverskin

CHAPBOOK
in memory of Jim Simmerman (1952-2006)

Reading
your poems
tonight I can
hear your voice reading
the lines, your voice pausing
as you used to, the rhythm
repeating, the line shattering my smooth breath.
I can see your mouth moving, your hand
bent like a branch and I never knew why.

Six or seven nights I have dreamed of you
and we're talking and you're alive but talking
about dying. Awake I drive up to
your house, or pause before your
office door, awake I remember
you saying the word
blueberries and how
I brought
them.

CLONMEL, 30 MAY 1992
for Niall

I saw a man tonight whose face held the shadows like yours.
but he was fairer in hair and older, too—
I wished it were you sitting there just ahead of me
in this old hall near the Suir.

To be with you here in Ardfinnan,
to listen to his great heart-music until we were tired,
to walk home through puddles along the dark road
under calm dripping trees.
Back in the small room,
we climb slowly into the cool bed.
To lie there together beneath the coverlet
and see the rain on the window—
O the smell of the breeze as it blows through,
a whispered, slow aire from the alley below.

To wake before dawn
and run down laughing
to the river and dive in
(shhh, it's Sunday)
but with the silver water so cold,
it's hard not to scream.

The sun is rising.
Wrapped in blankets,
we watch the golden light creep over the green.
The birds begin their Sunday songs
and the hills are quiet beyond us.

DIAMONDS HEAT THE HOUSE

What you have
is exactly what
I'm always looking for, he said.
How soon can you
come by? Monday's good,
I said.

And there go the Victorian diamonds
worn twice in ten years.
The magnifying glass
says Russian. Undergrad
graduation gift (thank you,
Mom)—sold
for a Smith College deposit,
a little propane
in a hollow tank.
Long winter, little work.
Worth it.
Done.

And there go the wedding rings—
sweet crescent moon
with tiny diamond stars
sparkling on
both sides, whether
coming or going.
And the other
an enameled
bluegreen river,
miniature metaphor,
encircling
curved channel

carved through white gold.
I saved the two carat
sapphire for our son.
Cornflower blue, dreamy to me
but not blue enough
to be worth much, the man said.

Tonight I'm in the river,
basalt-hearted and quiet.
I'm holding my breath
and from under
the churned surface
I see two children
standing on the shore.

DIGGING IN THE BINS
à la Heaney

Alluvial fan of coffee grounds,
sprouted-grain tortilla crusts,
rinds of goat cheese, rooibosch tea bags,
stalks of rainbow chard
and what are these?
Odd paper skins of tomatillos.
Little green tips from serrano chiles.
A wet plastic bag
containing tiny crumbs of broccoli.

Student loan statements, postcards
from London, "Love, Mom."
Endless *New Yorker* renewal squares
(under the bed, too).
Folks still use molasses?
No beer or wine bottles. Hmm.
Giant jugs of apple juice, little caper jar, that's it.
Her kid sure eats a ton of macaroni and cheese.

A-ha! A small sheaf of poems.
Hey here's one where she's in bed,
and not alone. Good news, heh heh.
But what's all this about the nightgown?
A pile of em about Ireland.
Narrow escapes.
Motherhood, breastfeeding. A treeclimber kid.
She's naked in this one! Who is John Henry Waddell?
Hey, you hear that? Someone wearing too-big boots and
    whistling.
Shit, here she comes.

DITCHING SCHOOL

1. Driving the 101

A burst of blackbirds overhead.
The music of their flight
pulls me into henna grass
along the road's edge, into tufts
of purple thistles.
I breathe warm green hills
not yet sunburned but soon, stretch my legs
under the broad and dark oaks my father loves
near the central coast of California.
From the blue bed of my pickup
I watch birds swing perfect
with the currents from cars
like my brother Pat on the waves at Windansea.

2. Easter, San Francisco

Marin slopes wide like Wicklow,
but where are the sheep?
"I've got to go home," Aidan sighs,
and stays silent til dusk.
He needs a drink
and his mates from Dublin, a deep bowl
of Joe's soup from Glendalough.
Pints at the Plough and Stars are for us
perfect medicine. Later
when the drum stops, Seamus steps
down from the wooden stage
to dance with me slow, pulls off
his silly black Australian hat

and we dance alone in the back,
back behind Randal's low fiddle, our slow shadows
drift across faded dartboards and empty kegs,
blue dress glides loose across my knees, my thoughts
resting on a stranger's shoulder, my heart
in my pocket, half inside-out.

DREAMLIFE

We'll never mow the grass, hardly ever
rake the leaves. Adopt a goat for the lawnmowing
and squirt her milk into strong tea.
Rainy days we'll build birdhouses
with daffodil views, sip nettle soup
three times each spring
as you grow into the Aran cardigan
handed down from Helen
and from Sarah before that.

Blackberries sleep tight in quilted jars,
sand whispers between summer sheets
and fairy milk's left on the sill, reflecting night
as moonlit clothes snap
out on the line, extended
under stars.

EIGHTH FLOOR
Grosvenor House Hotel, London

Up here

we're

eye to eye

with seagulls

FEBRUARY FIFTH
after Frank O'Hara

icicles melting
everywhere! mud puddles
beneath horsehooves!
pine needles floating
across clouds reflected!
and hot chocolate still the thing

FOR PATRICK

O Scantron, swimming pool, poolhall genius!
All-American alcoholic,
heroic heartbreak, my brother.
How to fit
your surfer's shoulders,
your red '66 Bonneville, your relapses,
Jesuit diplomas and scholarships, trips to the pawnshop,
your sandy feet, your discreet knightly manner
and magnificent grin,
your seven-hundred-dollar hotel bar tab
in London last Christmas,
your off-the-ground and holy bearhugs
with tattooed forearms, all shamrocks, sparrows and saints,
and your secrets, submerged
beneath quicksilver tears
and all that cheap beer—
how to fit you, little brother,
into this poem?

I'd love to write an ode as lyrical as you are,
moving through water with ball or board.
The formal, elevated style of an ode fits you perfectly
like a tuxedo or Speedo. You're dangerous
in either one; ask any one of my friends.
But let's get back to the poem
and its dignified theme
which, in this case, is death.
Tonight I'm awake late,
afraid you might really die,
that the drink might pull you finally under
like the ocean does her lovers sometimes.

You were born just before my first birthday.
I once could outrun you and later
outdrink you but not for long.
I really don't know you, the kid
across the teeter-totter
or the dinner table, napkins in our laps,
the kid behind me, holding tight to my T-shirt
astride the pony's back. I don't know
the serious man in the black motorcycle jacket
across the airplane aisle, reading a good magazine.
I don't know you,
I cannot put you back on the pony,
can't fit you into three stanzas,
can't save you.

GHOST FAMILY, SWEET POND ROAD
Guilford, Vermont

If you slice
the house
horizontally
like a layered cake
three times
but through the center
of the rooms
and then listened
eyes closed
listened with your nose
listened with your collarbones
listened past the rising yeast
of your fear

you'll hear
the other family
the ghost family
who shares this house

I heard them one day
while alone and dozing

We coexist

They are a new discovery

I will get back to you
on how it goes

So far, so good

GRADUATE SCHOOL

For our next assignment, I will write
the most beautiful poem ever written.
The world catches wind of it
and I cannon-ball into the literary scene.
Offers and invitations fill my tilted rusty mailbox.
Embossed envelopes tumble and sprawl out in the gravel
along the sloping road's rough edge.

The handsome boy in my class speaks to me,
the quiet, clever one with a hero's name,
those broad climber's shoulders and lyrical hands,
the one who always wears green.
He invites me to his slouching eastside house
and I take all his green clothes off
one rainy afternoon soon and I ride him
on his mattress on the floor.
He's delicious, better than I envisioned—
That's just one thing great poems are for.

THE HEAT WAVE II

Like sand she disappeared beneath the water,
all quiet, save the rustling of the hare
in yellow leaves. She was her mother's daughter;
her hair, it floated out, toes in the air.

All quiet, save the rustling of a hare,
the blue dress rested over boughs.
Her long hair floated out, her toes came up for air.
The black dog sighed in mud as cool as dawn.

A blue dress gently billowed in cottonwood boughs.
From hollow reeds, a call rose from the frog
deepdown in mud as cool as dawn. The black dog
sighed, muddy-bellied, his dark eyes blink-blinked.

No call rose from the frog in hollow reeds.
All was quiet, save the rustling of the hare.
Dark-eyed, he rested muddy-bellied
in yellow leaves. Deepdown she was her mother's daughter.

HOME BIRTH IN A BLUE BEDROOM
for Avery

We had the walls painted blue
not because we knew you were a boy
but to invite blue's cool and calm inside.
A powder blue sail or the sky
blue over the ocean—
something like that.

And when you came through
I rocked atop the plank floors,
leaning into the blue
walls, windows open, white sash
splashed with raindrops.

Lying on my side in the near-dark,
the hardest part—
I rode each cresting wave as you
moved closer to our shore.
I felt as never before
interior white pelvic bones
and then
you swooshed
into the room,
into the midwife's freckled arms
gasping, everyone gasping.
An oceanic moment,
thunderstorms,
almost midnight.

HOW DID YOU KNOW

The lamps are full, the woodbox, too.
The clocks have fallen back to mark the darkness.

There's evidence of presence,
    daughters, neighbors.
A glow, true heat. Bread and fruit and tea.

She's watched over by these portraits
that surround her on her nest (the couch):
    her former selves
        and ravens, roses, lilies, gulls.

You wouldn't know to see her now
or maybe yes you would.
The glimmer is deeper in her,
    the blue, the blue
        goes all the way through.

How many of Richard's cameras rest inside that cabinet?
And all the lenses pointing up the hill.
The apple and the pear tree,
    long limbs of lovely Sadie
        rows of shining scopes unblinking.

And still here—flashes in the red stove and in our dreams
Bright blast of recognition
    O tincture on the tongue
Delicately painted—her name, then framed!

The ornate V of Verandah curves
        like a cross between
                the flower and the moon
and the woman that she is
tonight, here on the couch
wearing teal green
and brass and gold
        at seventy.

for Verandah Porche on the occasion of her 70th birthday
and in celebration of her Ellen McCulloch Lovell Award
in Arts Education from the Vermont Arts Council

I saw the word H O P E
spelled out in two
dancers' bodies
holding one shape.
All at once all
the letters appeared.
Maybe I've been
watching too much
Sesame Street or maybe
reading what I need
to read but I saw
the word H O P E all
in one pas de deux.
All the angles and corners
overlayed, a palimpsest
of letters, limbs,
reminding me (knees
elbows toes shoulders
chins necks hands cheek
bones) reminding me
that the alphabet
breath bent over
and clasped
holds the moment
before the upright gasp.

in response to Karole Armitage's Ligeti Essays from the Vermont Performance Lab's Club trip to Boston's ICA, October 2013

IN THE BUZZING COUNTRY
for Kingman B. IV

Today and often lately I long for the dark green cool
of a big New England pond: trillium, turtles,
tired children resting belly-down on faded towels,
strawberry-stained and muddy. Highways home
lush with trees whose names I haven't learned.
Rolling along unpaved backroads, bare feet
on the dusty dash of someone else's car.

Horses munch spicy buttercups and swat deerflies
out in fields behind the house.
Dragonflies hover and zip
over iris and sunflowers standing tall
amid billowing beds of romaine and basil at sunset.

Candlelit nights in the buzzing country,
drinking tea with honey late around the long table,
breathing in the faces and voices of friends I'm never full of,
the friends that just know what I mean
as frogs, crickets, the whole world hums
just outside the old screen door.

LONG WEEKEND SHORTS

I. Thursday afternoon at a quarter-past-three
G and I, we shot out west on the I-40
to California.
drove the high road for a change,
sunset in our eyes,
turkey and avocado sandwiches in our laps
and gasoline—
three dollars and seventy-nine cents a gallon!

II. The Milky Way never so fresh, a spray
of soft white mystery and we're part of it
blasting down smooth highway
past new neon, tractors and two-syllable towns:
Amboy, Kelso, Ludlow, Barstow.
(Didn't notice Needles, still reeling
in that greenriversmell that came before.)

III. El Sereno is serene tonight, we've got
uninterrupted Mozart streaming in
and steaming Earl Grey at midnight
all the way from Sainsbury's.
My best girl Rachel's at her desk. I've lost her
to law school. But between kid-art and Kitty TV,
cheese & crackers & jar of bright pepperonccinis,
I'm good, I'm full. I'm home.

IV. At breakfast with Jack I notice
he's whiskered like I'm freckled.
Over omelettes, waffles and bad coffee we pingpong
between his new screenplay and my first story.
You know, I still love Kerouac, I admit.
His flow and the panorama, his observation.

That's benzedrine, Jack says
as the waitress slides the check.
Outside on the South Pasadena sidewalk
he gifts me a fine old hunting jacket, velvety pigskin
the color of Malibu sand and lined
in tomato-red satin. Ooooooeeeeee.
It doesn't fit me anymore, he says.
I bought it with John Huston
when I was shooting *Escape from Alcatraz*.
It'll keep you warm out there
in the mountains.

V. Heading home along the high desert diagonal,
a freight train in the distance
is a beaded belt
wrapped round the hips
of the mountain: white, rust, red and blue.

VI. Ocotillo alleluia, unblossomed in October,
the longest green arms outstretched up, up, up
and pointing east
towards the peaks, pointing back west
towards the dark ocean, reaching this way
and that. Home is here
in this blue pickup on this quiet highway right now,
my daughter's head on my lap and her dreams
rising past me, blown out the window
to drift between the night sky
and the earth like dandelion, whooooosh!
Home is here
and home's behind us, home
also waits up ahead: the honey jar,
the clothesline, our books and cats,
the well-made bed.

LOVE POEM TO ME
(she dared me)

curled up with your rosyboy asleep beside you
reading late by headlamp, snuggled down
in your dead grandfather's cardigan
ragged blue Scottish cashmere full of holes
you smell minty, lemony
or like wet roses, clean

your prayers interrupt the pages turning
your tears for the suffering of strangers
our holy human family
you dream of grandmother trees
honeybee alphabets, your true love
you love through pain
across miles like a rainbow
the hum is always there
high frequency

i love you
i don't need to change you
you give a shit, you're golden
i need you around
humming along on task
or laughing, cartwheeling, whistling
shuffling off to Buffalo
dreaming up your future
breathing and grateful, praying
your wordless hum of pure love
making soup and baking bread

rest your head, dear one
climb into the pocket of God's favorite shirt
just for this moment, rest your head
you are so loved

MORNINGS FULL OF SUNLIGHT

I.

When you are old, I want to be old
and still here. I don't want to miss
any of you, though I already do.

Little bowls of breakfast—ramekins
with a small bamboo spoon. Jamjars of milk
and your vitamins. Brushing your
hair to the side, golden light
of July in each strand, it's wild.

2.

All of this will end—mornings
full of sunlight. I once walked
to school with my two younger brothers.
We balanced like a tricycle, we
didn't tip until we got too big.
We rode unpaved backroads
no headlamps
and we made it through
somehow/how?

3.

Tonight
the mother part of me wishes
I could go back
to those three and say
God I know it's been so scary!
Please come out from under the manzanita

MY DAUGHTER'S HAIR

I haven't yet been able to find words—
a sentence for what happens when I brush
my daughter's hair and divide into thirds
enough hair for a family of four
(one barber said, the rare one I trusted).
Honeycomb-colored braid, she's out the door
for school (green coat, pink backpack), and rushing
right on time, little Virgo, to the bus.

One-woman-show with harmonies, alone—
amazed, bowed down (deep inhale) O the joy
contained in waves on waves: a shimmering song
my daughter's hair sings as she floats
each afternoon high up into a tree.
Against the clouds she climbs, far beyond me.

NAKED LADY
(Amaryllis Belladonna)

Leafless, her pink star head atop a foot-tall stalk,
leaning where you least expect bulbs to bloom:
alleyways, gravel edges of gas stations, laundromats.
I've seen her bloom beside steel poles bearing street signs,
on a hill at the edge of town, and out back of my house.
Naked Lady.

Her scent is the thing, unbelievable.
She's more than tough and pretty—
she catches the light.
And when your nose pokes inside her bell,
that feathery sugarflower breath
makes you want to blow a bubble.
Imagine the pink ice cream flavor: NAKED LADY

Longlegged, pink hat-headed Naked Lady,
my kind of girl, backroads and railroad yards.
Dishwater rainspout survivor. Beautiful,
leaning against old houses in her bare feet,
out beneath my California clotheslines,
bordered by midnight raccoon/possum/skunkpath,
tomato plant forest.

She's there at the edge of town, *most obscenely*
and courageously leaning naked
at all hours in her perfect pink hat.
You can't miss her.

NEO-MONASTIC

The convent
O she calls to me—

a convent of my own design:
on horseback in the Pampa
I will be
under widest sky
with the Mystery
in Good's time

O my heart

new moon over wing mountain and i'm driving towards it, towards the pink sunset and jagged black outlines of ponderosas all along the plateau, all up and over and down, black against pink and my blue truck hums along the yellowstripe road, camouflaged with the sky, blue square of mirror and one blue eye. above me first stars blink in the rainbow sherbet sunset. driving home singing towards wing mountain, towards my house leaning back green against ponderosas in their volcanic bed with hummingbird visitors taking last sips before flying back to cacti in bisbee. new moon over wing mountain, this babyblue pickup passing last latesummer grasses and dandelions, new slivermoon low over wing mountain, ahead the ribboned sunset, white wisp of new moon caught in the weft and sentences of clouds written overhead, yes.

ODE TO GAIL CARTER DEMAINE

Perennially you
smiled with your whole body
and strode longlegged
into life. Even later
with your canes, climbing hills,
always forward.
A human sequin: purple, gold and blue.
A tall elf in tennis shoes.

The day I met you, summer shone
in the trees and on your face.
A strange gold shape hung from your neck
on a chain—Martha's Vineyard,
you later explained. I pictured you
with David and your beautiful sons,
eating blackberries, barefoot in the sand.
For girls far from home, you were mother
to many those years in Crossley;
you were our lighthouse.

You believed in people with motherforce,
reflecting our light back to us.
You were a torch held high.
Who could not be buoyed
by your bright beam?
No small gift for any teen or friend,
adrift or slicing through currents.
At some point, every one of us
needs someone
waving on the shore.

I have never been one
to believe in Heaven, but now
I hope for a place
where I might meet you
and again say *thank you, Gail, thank you*—
a place where the sun
warms your dear dark head.

OÍCHE SHAMHNA / NOVEMBER'S EVE
for McAleer

Over and over
like a train following tarred ties—
your fierce music,
burning as you bend
harmonious with sunset.
The cracks are nearly filled:
this room, the saucer,
the unmailed letter
of my heart.
Tea stains are invisible
by candlelight.

You now across the sea
and me wishing
I could ring you but
it's dawn in Gweedore
and you're sleeping.

Your hands, imprinted on my shoulder,
Your Northern voice, a corkscrew
in my hair, a swarm of bees inside my chest.
Your skull rests
on the ocean floor
here in the blue bowl of my hips.

For you I'd sit with any pencil
and this falling—
a poem rising every night.
For you a wish goes out
across red-tiled rooftops
across the silver skin

of the Pacific Ocean and up
to stars
to one cold, unnamed moon
that pulls all things,
sand/water/blood
and light,
without boundary, border
or destination, without obstacle.

OUR SUNDAY SONG

1. Out

The aspen's golden
coins sparkle; my daughter says
It sounds like water.

The brown and white paint
grazes in the long red grass
and October wind.

2. In

I nap in jeans, she reads,
both under soft blankets,
rushing wind outside.

We wish for these things:
a fireplace, two horses,
a room just for books.

PICKUP

        I   call   her
       my   other
daughter my baby   blue
Ford F150 Safe   blue enclosed world Safe for first tears
sharing the bench seat with carseat best friends or with lovers
Kisses atop the blue plastic plaid Tailgate sandwiches best in the
     world I mean   it delish
     ripest tomato   avocado
     windows 360   openheart . . .

POCKET

And I'm here again
hanging out in the pocket
of God's favorite shirt

in worn blue flannel
filtered light and sound
I'm suspended
along for the ride

Tag-along, tiny human
I am held and warm
horizontal against heartbeats
I can't see the sky

SINGING AT MATT MALLOY'S
Westport, County Mayo

And afterwards when
sober, red-faced uncles
grabbed me for a dance,
that freedom
I've always been chasing
was mine and I hung on (eyes
closed against the tourists)
whirling round the center,
grinning as we flew
and stomped just so.
The music roared in my head
like the fierce hum of sea
inside a shell—salty
and unending
and for long moments
I was entirely possessed
by that ordinary magic.

SINGLE MOM AND BABY SPEND BIRTHDAY
IN BED WITH VIRUS

Sky thick with clouds. The baby yawns vomit
Onto cotton sheets. I blink at the sink,
Think (my dad's voice), "Looks like a bomb hit
Ya." Had I the choice, I'd tuck in and drink

The day, but smile sweet as new corn
Keeps deep blues at bay. Angel's tray: gold tea,
Warm raisins in bread, butter—I'm reborn
Times twenty-three. Any regrets? Not me.

Blue feverish eyes peek out. Though not near dead,
She's roasting in the bed. Half-moon dimple,
Two teeth on the horizon and hair red
Though mine is dark and his is black, simple.

Her fathers' eyes shine up with feverfire.
I'd kick him if he walked in now, liar!

SNAP

We each took a photograph at the edge of the sea
that day. Only the one he snapped of G and me remains:
we're squinting into the Irish sun, a wise-
cracker star who shows up for an hour and disappears.
The clouds over there have a knack for closing
the curtains. They swallow the sunlight up.

My navyblue baby and I shivered on the dock: up-
turned faces, ocean, sky. In the photo you see
the dark tower of his shadow across the planks, close
to our feet. I remember swans drifting down the main
channel of the Shannon, whiteness merging, disappearing
into the sun's glare. I wrapped all my whys

inside my black wool coat, cinched the wide
sash, said goodbye. *Seeyeh at The Red Rose at sunup,*
he said. At breakfast he wasn't the man from the pier,
but hunched and silent over rashers and tea.
His broken promise to me—a dark stain
down the front of his proud soldier's coat.

That last morning, we wore Sunday's clothes,
she in brightly striped tights, little red shoes. *Why'd
this happen? What'll I tell her?* The pain
round that table sealed all my vessels up.
He turned from us, rose from his seat
to leave us for good. A white wave of fear

crashed over me as he disappeared.
The bell jingled cheerfully, the cafe door closed.
I should have let him go, you see.
What happened next, worse than broken promises. The sky,
as they say, was changeable. Outside, he up
and agreed to a drive, seven miles of cloud, pulled off the main

road, down a long track through trees. The mane
of my hair covered our child. He cut the engine, disappeared,
I thought, for a pee. Perfect, I actually said and up
I stood with my dozing armful. He swept in close
from nowhere, his fist flat on my mouth. Bam-bam, twice
and away. My books flew hard from car windows, aimed at me.

No photos remain of my daughter's father at the sea-
shore. I have stopped wondering where or why.
I once soaked the bruised door of that story with whiskey
til it closed. Still the magic words have not appeared.

SNOWED IN

It's mid-March and the first real snow is falling.
I have learned to make a good fire since he left
(though unsure how I'll pay all the rent).
Still this life is beautiful right down to the dog.
My daughter's a pearl reflecting all manner of light.
Flute-player, shepherd-walker, she disappears for days
into great big books. Today in the sun
we kept busy with seeds, feeding all the little birds
in our far gusty corner of the meadow; it was Finch TV til sunset.

One red-breasted flyer crashed into our window at noon.
I brought him inside, held him two-handed
as his spirit landed back into his little brown body, and me
imagining miniature cartoon stars
whirling in a halo round his trembling head.
He shat twice in my hand, blinking.
Eventually and back outside, he flew away
audibly and at a tilt towards some scattered seeds
like a tiny feathered jetplane.

O Creator of snowflakes, finches and pearls,
I surrender. I wish to drift again
in your grace as a feather does: useful and light,
part of a miraculous wing.

If only I could pry out the pain and skip it,
frozen, far across a dark lake
like a stone.

SOBER THANKSGIVING WITH STRAYS

Kevin combed his nest of hair
Megan baked a pie
Casey telephoned his kids and had a public cry

Bellnda brought a brand-new game
Judy read our palms
Nancy roasted everything and set off no alarms

Gráinne teased the grownups
Cindy hushed them for the prayer
Judy thanked God standing up
And God was everywhere

SPRING IN THE FIRST FLOOR WOMEN'S
BATHROOM AT NORTHERN ARIZONA UNIVERSITY

What a shame to zip
French cherry-blossomed panties
back into work pants.

Wish I could cartwheel,
just cotton hiphuggers, boots,
white linoleum.

TOUCHING THE GROUND
Islandeady, County Mayo

The coconut breath of yellow whinbushes
rushed through the Opel's open windows
as we sped past cows and clouds
and abandoned stone cottages.

Crunching gravel, we turned left
off the narrow road and parked
beside a new bungalow,
built onto a century-old twin of itself.

A tiny woman wearing crow's ragged blacks
and her dead husband's cap
led us out walking west through her fields,
her cheeks bright as a newborn's.
The hems of our skirts were soon wet
from the clover.

She knelt easily in the grass like a young girl,
brushed her hand along the cracked foundation's edge.
Here it is, she said.
The old O'Brien house stood here. Ages ago.
I bent down beside her, my hair
tumbled out of its knot,
whisking the flecked grey mortar.
Hands pressed into the ground, I smelled
the turf smoke of wet west of Ireland nights
in the damp wool of her cap.
A linnet's song came from the hill
as behind us my aunt smiled
into the ever-moving clouds.

TWO ODES

1. Clothespin
your wooden legs
snap shut
unless
wads of cotton
bunch in your crotch

Headless, modern,
a steel stripe
up your stockings,
all legs,
like an Irish dancer

2. Outdoor Shower
falling water, wooden floor and walls
trees, clouds, and me
getting clean, steam
rising straight into sky

WALKING RAIN

billowing pillow clouds

clouds with skin, holding in

breathing out

walking rain

WINTER POLAROIDS FROM VERMONT

I love an orange bed
of coals: the basement's
glowing casserole

O cardinal!
I thought you were
a red leaf falling

CPSIA information can be obtained
at www.ICGtesting.com
Printed in the USA
LVOW11s2116060117

519786LV00005B/6/P

9 780996 897396